Days with the Universal Mother

tava kathāmṛtaṁ tapta jīvanaṁ
kavibhirīḍitaṁ kalmaṣapahaṁ
śravaṇamangalaṁ śrīmatātataṁ
bhuvi gṛṇanti te bhurida janaḥ

The nectar of your excellences revives the scorched spirit of mankind.
It purifies the sinner while holy men live on it.
To hear it is itself auspicious and peace generating.
They are the real gift makers who spread your name far and wide.

Śrīmad Bhagavatam 10.31.9

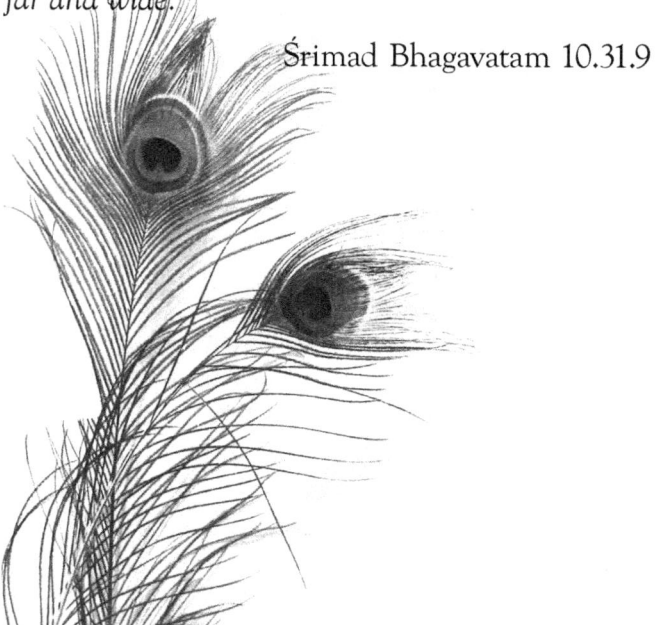

DAYS WITH THE UNIVERSAL MOTHER

Volume One

Swamini Atmaprana

Days with the Universal Mother
Swamini Atmaprana

Published by:
   Mata Amritanandamayi Center
   P.O. Box 613
   San Ramon, CA 94583
   United States
   www.amma.org

First edition: October 2017

Copyright © 2017 by Mata Amritanandamayi Center, P.O. Box 613, San Ramon, CA 94583, United States

All rights reserved No part of this publication may be stored in a retrieval system, transmitted, reproduced, transcribed or translated into any language, in any form, by any means without the prior agreement and written permission of the publisher.

In India:
   www.amritapuri.org
   inform@amritapuri.org

In USA:
   amma.org

In Europe:
   www.amma-europe.org

Contents

Dedication	7
Amma – The Doctor of Doctors	9
Visa to the Supreme Goal	15
Amma – the Mother of the Universe	21
Amma – the Shower of Immortality	25
Amma – the Ocean of Spiritual Power	33
Amma – the Supreme Teacher	37
Amma – the Cosmic Healer	43
Om Gāna-lolupāyai Namah	49
Amma – Dhyāna-dhyātṛ-dhyeya-rūpā	57

Dedication

oṁ paramātma svarūpiṇīṁ
mātṛ rūpa manoharīṁ
amṛtānandamayīṁ tvāṁ
pranamāmi muhurmuhuḥ

O, my Divine Mother, the reality of all that exists, the Mother of the whole world who attracts all beings with love and makes everyone happy, let me prostrate at your lotus feet again and again.

With humble prostrations I offer this book at my Guru's holy feet, and my thanks to all the friends who have given their invaluable service in preparing it.

> Lokāḥ Samastāḥ Sukhino Bhavantu.
> *May the whole world attain everlasting peace and happiness*

In Service to Amma,
Atmaprana
April 2017, Amritapuri

Oṁ Amṛteśwaryai Namaḥ

Chapter One

Amma – The Doctor of Doctors

Amma (Sri Mata Amritanandamayi Devi) graciously allowed me to join the ashram as a brahmacharini (female disciple) in 1985. At that time, Amma allotted the ashramites one hour daily for routine service and the remaining time for other spiritual practices. As I had been serving as a doctor, Brahmachari Nealu (later known as Swami Paramatmananda) handed over the first-aid box to me. In due course, devotees started bringing medicines. Amma enabled me to arrange these medicines in a small room. I dispensed the medicines to local patients and ashramites as needed.

Amma's parents, Damayanti Amma and Sugunanandan Acchan, were very affectionate and helpful to the ashramites. Damayanti Amma used to plait coconut leaves to make ashram huts and taught the ashramites many such household skills. Sometimes Damayanti Amma and I collected firewood for the ashram kitchen from the coconut yard. When the ashramites fell sick, she gave herbal medicines that she prepared herself. It was Damayanti Amma's habit to cook *payasam* (Indian sweet dish) with utmost care to offer to Amma during *Devi Bhava darshan* (the mood of the Divine Mother). On special occasions she cooked rice and worshipped the sun early in the morning and distributed the *prasad* (consecrated offerings blessed by Amma) to all.

Once, when Amma was on an international tour, Damayanti Amma fell down and had to be hospitalised. Since she was staying in a separate house with the family, I came to know of it only after a few days. Immediately, I rushed to the medical college hospital in Alappuzha where Damayanti Amma was undergoing treatment. On reaching the hospital, I found out that she had already undergone two surgeries. The first surgery was for the complicated bone fractures of the right arm. Though she withstood the first surgery, unfortunately, following it, she developed paralysis of the intestines. Her abdomen was distended and she was in great distress. The second surgery was conducted for correcting the abdominal problem. I saw Damayanti Amma lying in a semi-conscious state after the second surgery. Dr. Bhaskaran, a professor in the Orthopaedics Department and a devotee of Amma, had done the first surgery and had attended to the needs of Damayanti Amma during the second surgery. When he saw me, he entrusted the responsibilities to me, and thereafter he could render valuable service whenever required.

I joined Amma's younger brother Sateesh, who was at Damayanti Amma's bedside day and night, to take care of her. Though the gangrenous part of the intestine had been removed during the operation, Damayanti Amma's abdominal condition did not show any improvement. The stomach and intestines were totally functionless.

In spite of the maximum efforts taken by the doctors, Damayanti Amma's condition was deteriorating day by day. Since she could not take any solid food or liquids by mouth, she was sustained on continuous intravenous drips. I was using veins one after another for the IV drips. All the major veins of the arm were made use of. Damayanti Amma tolerated everything with a smile.

In addition to the critical abdominal condition, Damayanti Amma was diagnosed as diabetic and was treated for it. Since the hospital did not have sufficient facilities, Sateesh went to get necessary tests done in private laboratories. Though one month passed by, and all the veins in the arm – even very small veins – were used up for the drips, Damayanti Amma's condition did not improve.

Next, we started to use veins of the legs for giving drips. Praying to Amma, I used to sit close to Damayanti Amma, holding her feet to protect the IV line. After a few days, the last vein also collapsed and no more IV drips were possible. In this critical condition I prayed, *"Amma, medical science has failed to restore Damayanti Amma's health. Your children have become totally helpless; now you are our sole refuge. O, Divine Mother, you are the Doctor of doctors, kindly be gracious and shower your mercy on us!"*

Amma heard our intense prayer. Soon, to our great relief, we saw signs that Damayanti Amma's intestines were functional again. Distention of the abdomen was lessening. Doctors advised us to give water and fluids orally in very small amounts. Afterwards, solid food was also given. Digestion became satisfactory and Damayanti Amma's condition improved rapidly. With Amma's Grace, Damayanti Amma regained normal health and we soon returned to the ashram.

This miraculous event made an unforgettable impression in my mind.

Oṁ Namaḥ Śivāya

Oṁ Amṛteśwaryai Namaḥ

Chapter Two

Visa to the Supreme Goal

Amma initiated me into monastic life in 1994 and sent me for public service in various places in Kerala. I started doing house visits and conducted public programs, including Vilakku Pujas, in Trissur District. During the *puja* (ritualistic worship), the beautiful, lighted sacred lamp, called *Vilakku* in Malayalam, is symbolically worshipped as the Divine Mother. Fresh flowers are offered with the chanting of each of the 108 mantras describing Amma, followed by the Lalitā Sahasranāma, the Thousand Names of the Divine Mother. Though the Vilakku Puja and the Thousand Names are very well known and have been used by many

Indian families, Amma has widely rejuvenated the chanting of the Lalitā Sahasranāma in Kerala and throughout India, and has introduced it all over the world wherever she has travelled.

Once while I was engaged in public service in Trissur, I conducted a Vilakku Puja in a devotee's home. As I had witnessed many pujas in Amma's holy presence, I could give appropriate directions for conducting the puja at their house. The participants were divided into small groups, and to each group a sacred lamp, flowers and other necessary items for the puja were given. The devotees did the puja themselves. While doing the puja they could attain a higher mental state, and it was a unique experience for them to relieve their day-to-day worries and tensions. After the puja, I distributed the puja prasad to one and all.

At that time, a young woman named Seeta approached me and started to converse with me, shedding tears. Her husband, Kumaran, was running a business in Mumbai. Though the business was initially flourishing, after some time he was forced to close it down and come back home due to heavy loss. He started ill-treating Seeta, telling her that she was totally responsible for all the misfortune. Every day he returned home completely drunk and abused her. She could not bear this drastic change in her husband's character, and life became a great misery for the entire family.

Not knowing what to do, one day while Seeta was passing by a temple, with Amma's grace, she happened to see a photograph of Amma. Immediately she entered the temple and enquired whether she could participate in any of Amma's programs there. They told her, "The photograph is kept here as a token of devotion to Amma; presently, programs are being conducted by Her disciples in Thrissur." She told me that somehow she managed to reach the house in time to meet me. On hearing Seeta's sad story, I prayed to Amma for her and gave her the offered flowers and sacred ash as Amma's prasad, and told her how to use them daily. I also stressed the necessity of incessant remembrance of Amma. I advised her to surrender herself to Amma, the Divine Mother, and pray intensely. She returned home with great relief and started a spiritual life. Her two children also joined her. As I had advised, the prasad was kept in the puja room, and in due course a remarkable change could be noticed in her husband's nature. He gradually stopped the consumption of liquor and started to give Seeta money for household expenses. His attitude towards his wife and children changed, and scolding and beating stopped.

Kumaran decided to go to one of the Gulf countries to take up a job there. Seeta's brother gave him sufficient money to meet the travel expenses. Seeta and Kumaran requested me to conduct a spiritual program in their house on the day before his departure to Mumbai, where he would go to secure his visa. Unfortunately, that day a *harttal* (strike) was announced. Vehicles were not allowed to ply on the road. Yet with Amma's blessings, the *bhajan group* (devotional singers) and I reached the house in the evening in time. The program consisted of a short spiritual discourse by me, singing of bhajans and distribution of prasad. It went very well, and an atmosphere of happiness and contentment prevailed in the family. Following this, they had an intense yearning to meet Amma in Amritapuri. Though they could not do so, as Amma was on a foreign tour at that time, Seeta's husband became closely devoted to Amma inwardly.

The next day Kumaran left for Mumbai. He expected that a gentleman in Mumbai, whom he considered his friend, would help him. Kumaran gave him the money needed to procure the visa, but his friend cheated him and withheld his visa, demanding more and more money from him. Seeta informed me of this predicament and requested my guidance. I advised her to pray to Amma and wait, and not to quarrel with that man. With Amma's blessings, soon Seeta's husband was able to come into contact with a good-hearted Arab. The man was impressed by Kumaran's work skills, and sponsored his visa. He took him to Saudi Arabia and enabled him to get a suitable job there.

Day by day the condition of Seeta's family improved because of her husband's financial help. Her children were able to study in good schools. They had extra money to purchase a cassette player, so they were able to learn many of Amma's recorded bhajans. Afterwards, Seeta invited me to organise several public programs and house visits in their village. Her children also accompanied me in singing bhajans during these house visits. Following Seeta's example, many people in the village became Amma's devotees and could solve their various problems.

After a few years, Kumaran returned home on leave. The whole family came to Amritapuri and had Amma's *darshan* (close interaction with Amma). Thus, Seeta's family, which was immersed in a sea of tears, could now enjoy peace and prosperity, by Amma's grace.

Devotion to Amma gives not only the ordinary visa, but also the "visa" to the Supreme Goal.

Oṁ Namaḥ Śivāya

Oṁ Amṛteśwaryai Namaḥ

Chapter Three

Amma – the Mother of the Universe

It was monsoon time during one of the early years of the ashram. Consequent to the continuous, heavy rainfall, the ashram yard and the nearby areas were covered with water. It looked as though Mother Earth was in a sound sleep under the thick blanket of rainwater. As the Bhava darshan was over, Amma was engaged in light conversation with the devotees and making arrangements for their stay in the ashram overnight.

When I came back to my hut after the Bhava darshan, I found that the roof had been leaking and water had collected on the floor. At that time, Doctor Devaki, who had come for Amma's darshan, happened to come there. She was a devotee of Amma and was close to me. Seeing that I had no place to sleep in my hut, she took me with her to her room and allowed me to sleep there. That was the only concrete building available for devotees who came for Bhava darshan. Many devotees were taking rest in that room, and I joined them.

Within a few minutes I heard Amma's divine voice calling me, "Leela mol" [darling daughter Leela]. Immediately I rushed out of the room, and was surprised to see Amma standing near the veranda. I felt sad to note that She had walked through knee-deep water to reach there. While accompanying Amma back to Her room, She told me that Her leg was cut by an iron wire floating in the water. On reaching Amma's room I examined Her and found a long wound on the right leg. I cleaned and dressed the wound with necessary medicines. Thereafter, Amma mentioned nothing about it. Instead, She affectionately asked me, "My child, why did you go there? You could have very well come to Amma's room." I could only remain spellbound thinking of Amma's all-flowing divine love. I felt so happy that I was going to spend the rest of the night in Amma's room. Amma had a light dinner and gave me the prasad. Thereafter, She started to take rest lying on the floor. I sat beside Amma, massaging Her holy feet.

With Amma's blessings, my mind was very calm and still, and remained immersed in Her. I could chant the mantra given to me by Amma incessantly and meditate on Her divine form. In the morning Amma woke up and asked me to examine Her wound. I removed the dressing to see how the wound was. To my great astonishment, I could not see any wound or any mark of the wound on Amma's leg! The skin appeared normal. I was unable to utter even a single word and sat totally silent. Amma started Her morning routine as though nothing had happened. It was quite obvious that the whole of Amma's divine play was to bring me close to Her and to make me realise that Amma's children would always have sufficient place in Her divine abode.

Amma, the Mother of the Universe, who is the Creator, Sustainer and Destroyer of the whole world, can make anything appear or disappear by Her own will. She was making me conscious of the fact that She is the sole refuge to Her children under all circumstances. In the years that followed, Amma gave me many similar divine experiences for my spiritual development and fulfilment of my ashram life.

Oṁ Namaḥ Śivāya

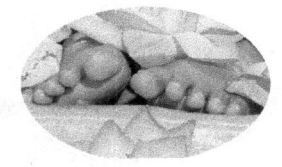

Oṁ Amṛteśwaryai Namaḥ

Chapter Four

Amma – the Shower of Immortality

It was May 1990, during the Installation festival of the Chennai Brahmasthanam Temple[1]. Amma was performing the installation (*prana pratistha*) Herself. People were suffering from the heat and severe scarcity of water in that scorching summer. The heat and thirst caused by the weather was in cruel contrast to the spiritual purity of the Brahmasthanam atmosphere. For seven days the Lalitā Sahasranāma was chanted five times per day, while Amma's

---

[1] A place for worshipping Brahman.

Divine presence, bhajans and darshan drew many people to the festival. These events were conducted to purify the atmosphere of the temple that would soon provide a refuge for the public to worship, meditate and perform pujas to overcome their misfortunes and suffering.

One of the week's events included a spiritual discourse by a well-known speaker, who, in the midst of his speech, recalled the following incident. Decades earlier, during a similar hot and dry summer, Sri Rajagopalachari, the eminent political leader, writer and spiritual exemplar, organised a *Japa Yajna* (the continuous chanting of God's name by a gathering of devotees). Following the Yajna, there was a heavy rain. As though challenging Amma, the speaker asked, "Can Amma also make it rain now, here in Madras?" The very next day there was a torrential downpour. Devotees felt that the unseasonal rain, which brought immense relief to the people of Madras, was a direct response to the speaker's challenging words.

Scriptures proclaim, and Amma personifies the fact, that selfless activities performed for the benefit of the world generate boundless divine energy, the vibrations of which reach the solar atmosphere and give rise to rainfall. Everyone was convinced that the seven-day program held in Amma's holy presence was the sole cause of the unexpected rain. During the return journey to the ashram, it was with prayerful joy and gratitude that the ashramites travelled in the buses, which had to be driven through the accumulated water on the roads.

During a similar scorching summer, Amma was invited to the city of Madurai. The memory of the programs in the hot summer of the previous years in Madurai made me think, "How can the ashram children withstand the extreme heat and scarcity of water there?" At first I petulantly felt that it would have been better if the programs were to be held at a more suitable time. "Amma is certainly beyond the dualities of heat and cold, but Her children have not yet reached that high state," I thought to myself. But the rapturous thought that we could travel with Amma, the Supreme Teacher, and be with Her in Madurai, brushed aside all such worries and anxieties.

Amma's programs were conducted at various public places in Madurai, including temples. Day programs included the Vilakku Puja, satsang and darshan, while evening programs included bhajans, darshan, and a few house visits. The last evening program of bhajans and Bhava darshan was held in an auditorium.

During the bhajans before Bhava darshan, as it was very hot, I came out of the auditorium and stood in a breeze in the courtyard, immersed in the bhajans. All of a sudden the sky became dark and cloudy. For a moment I thought that it might be due to the smoke from factories, but soon raindrops started to fall, followed by a heavy rain. The unexpected rainfall made it possible for me to sit happily near Amma the whole night serving Her during the Bhava darshan. I realised that Amma had given the heavy rain not only to reduce the extreme heat of the day, but also to relieve my anxiety. Amma who is beyond time and space, can rise above all unfavourable situations and protect us like a defensive shield.

A similar incident occurred in Trissur during our house visit campaign. As per Amma's divine instructions, we organised house visits in various areas of Trissur. With ashramites and local devotees, we conducted the house visits, called the *Amrita Sauhrda Yajna*. The aim was to bring Amma's message of love and compassion to the houses to enable the members of the family to live in peace and prosperity. Usually an average of twenty house visits went on from morning to evening. We had lunch and a short rest in one of the houses. Since the construction of the Trissur ashram building was in the starting stage, we stayed in the homes of devotees.

Though it was monsoon time, people suffered from lack of rain and scarcity of water. Once, when we were taking a short rest after lunch in a house, the mother of the house and a neighbouring woman approached me. They pointed out to me the severe scarcity of water and many related problems that they faced. They told me, "People ask us why is there no rain in spite of the house visits made by Amma's disciples." I thought for a moment and told them,

"We will have to pray to Amma continuously and wait." That night it rained heavily where we were staying and in the surrounding areas. In the morning, as we made our way to the next house visit in the neighbouring village, we walked through paths that were covered with water.

Amma, verily the Ocean of Compassion, can shower on us the rain of immortality. What we need is right understanding, and with that faith to offer ourselves at Her Holy Feet.

Oṁ Namaḥ Śivāya

Oṁ Amṛteśwaryai Namaḥ

Chapter Five

Amma – the Ocean of Spiritual Power

In the early years of my ashram life, I used to spend time with Amma in Her room almost every day. Once, after my morning routine (meditation, etc.), I went to Amma's room for darshan. Amma was advising an ashram resident who hailed from Switzerland. When he left, She asked me to sit close to Her. Amma was lying down on Her bed and wanted me to press either side of Her forehead. While doing so, I noticed that Amma was completely immersed in Her inner self and unconcerned with the outside world.

Amma, who is *Ātmārāmāgraganyā* ("the first and foremost among those who revel in the Higher Self"), remained totally motionless. As I continued to press Her forehead, my mind was elevated to a new experience. After some time, Amma asked me to massage Her right arm. I started to massage Her arm, but after a few seconds – to my astonishment – I found that my hand was not moving. The hand was stuck as if it were in contact with an electric line. When I saw that Amma was completely unconscious of the external world, I tried to massage my own left arm. I was convinced that my hand was moving normally. Again I tried to massage Amma's arm and found that, as before, my hand was not moving. I left my hand in that state on Her arm and started meditating. My mind became completely still, and, by Amma's grace, I could sit immersed in bliss for quite some time. When Amma got up after a long while, I related to Her what had happened. Amma replied that She had transmitted a wave of spiritual energy to me.

Amma, Ocean of Spiritual Power and Amritanandam [Eternal Bliss], kindly always give me your helping hand and save me from the ocean of *samsara* [worldly life] to make me blissful forever.

Years later, during a North Indian tour, through a similar experience Amma revealed to me the sanctity of *pada teertha* [holy water from the pada puja]. It was when Amma was received by the devotees at the venue of a public function. Usually we brahmacharinis followed Her closely on such occasions. I was not able to make my way through the crowd to be near Amma when the *pada puja* [the holy worship of Amma's feet] was done. By the time I reached the site, the whole pada puja was over, and She was proceeding to the stage along with devotees. It was my habit to drink a little of the holy water from the pada puja and put some over my head. I pondered for a moment whether I should skip using the pada teertha that day. Though Amma had almost reached the stage and I was away from Her, I did not want to break my good habit. I used the holy water as usual. As soon as I put it over my head, I obtained an unusual result. I stood there lost in a rare bliss and peace. I continued to be in that state of mind for a while. When I became conscious of the surroundings I rushed to Amma. I learned that a spiritual aspirant must not break good habits and has to be punctual in performing the routine.

Amma, may I prostrate again and again at your Holy Feet!

Oṁ Namaḥ Śivāya

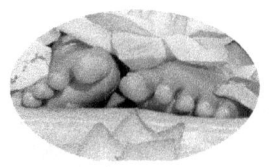

Oṁ Amṛteśwaryai Namaḥ

Chapter Six

Amma – the Supreme Teacher

On Amma's first visit to Mumbai, the brahmacharis and brahmacharinis [male and female disciples] also accompanied Her. Amma stayed in a devotee's home, and we stayed in several nearby houses. The brahmacharinis were pleased to stay in the home closest to Her. It was a two-storey building that belonged to a Punjabi family who generously vacated the entire first floor for our use.

Though I was in Amma's room most of the time, I went to the Punjabi family's house daily for my bath and meditation. The mother of the house

extended a very warm welcome to me every day. During our friendly conversations, she expressed her desire to know more about Amma's life and teachings. I tried my best to clear her doubts. As days passed by, I started thinking of her during my meditation and what more I could tell her about Amma.

One day when I went to Amma, I found Her giving darshan to a few devotees. I stood near Her to see if I could offer any service. After the devotees left, Amma prepared to go for the morning program. She unexpectedly turned to ask me, *"My child, nowadays in your meditation, three people are there, is it not?"* I thought to myself, I am sitting alone to meditate, but Amma says three are there. In a flash I realised that besides Amma and me – the ideal of meditation and the meditator – sometimes that kind lady of the house also appeared as the third person!

What Amma meant by Her question became quite clear. Thereafter when I meditated, I tried to fix my mind on Amma and the mantra [sacred words]. The awareness that Amma is the Supreme Teacher, who knows each and every thought of

Her disciples and guides them accordingly, filled my heart with ineffable joy.

Amma gave two programs per day during this first visit to Mumbai. The morning program included the Vilakku Puja and darshan, while the evening program consisted of bhajans, darshan, and a few house visits. Once, when Amma came back after the evening program it was nearing daybreak. Hearing the birds singing in the yard outside Amma's room, I told Her, "Amma, it is almost four o'clock in the morning, the birds are up and chirping." She responded by saying, *"My child, surely Amma is unconditioned by time."* I realised that Amma is the Inner Self who keeps vigil day and night.

After a while a new brahmachari came to Amma because he had heard that She was leaving for Her first western tour soon. He was on the verge of tears. Amma consoled him saying, "My son, in the western countries, many of Amma's children are also waiting for Me. In east or west, many people are engrossed in worldliness." Amma then cited the example of the little birds. These birds, forgetting that they can relish honey from the flowers, get immersed in the mud puddles nearby." She continued, "Amma must make them fly by clapping Her hands." The brahmachari's anxiety was instantly relieved when he heard Amma's nectarous words. He prostrated at Amma's feet and took leave of Her. I understood that Amma's mission in life is to uplift Her children from the whirlpool of worldliness towards the joys of Immortal Bliss.

Om̐ Namaḥ Śivāya

Oṁ Amṛteśwaryai Namaḥ

Chapter Seven

Amma – the Cosmic Healer

Once, when Amma was on a western tour, Susheela, an ashramite hailing from Switzerland, approached me and explained, "Leelakka [my pre-monastic name], I have a boil on my back. During my last Kodungalloor trip with Amma, I went to the hospital because I had a boil on my foot. The doctor incised the boil and removed the pus. Since the procedure was very painful and hard to tolerate, I have decided that I will not go to any hospital for such treatments hereafter. I request you to do what is needed to cure my present ailment."

I was in a dilemma as to how I could help Susheela, when I suddenly remembered the Amrita creeper, a very valuable medicine for many diseases. I had seen it growing in the ashram yard near Amma's parent's house. Unfortunately, when I looked for it, I could not find it. I thought Damayanti Amma, who was very fond of plants, might know where to find the creeper. When I asked her, she said that it might have been removed by mistake when the area was cleaned. When I looked again, to my great relief, I discovered a branch of the creeper hanging from a betel nut palm tree. (The Amrita creeper is capable of growing on trees even if its roots have been cut off.)

I quickly plucked a few leaves and rushed to Susheela's room. Spreading a suitable amount of milk-cream, I applied the leaf to the boil. When the first leaf dried up, I removed it and applied a new one. Daily I collected and applied two or three leaves. Within two days the boil opened up and the pus started to come out. Susheela's pain also subsided considerably. In due course, though the pus formation was less, the wound had not yet healed. It was with fervent prayers that I plucked and applied the last leaf. The next day, when I examined the wound, I was relieved to find that it had completely healed.

Susheela was very happy when I narrated the whole incident to her. Then she told me, "This time when we all wrote to Amma, I wrapped my letter[1] with a leaf from the holy banyan tree. Offering this very holy leaf to Amma made me very happy." I replied, "You offered a leaf to Amma, and She in return gave you the required number of leaves to cure your illness. Whatever we offer to Amma with devotion, She accepts, and showers Her blessings on us. If we offer our life itself to Amma, She will remove all our miseries and bestow eternal peace upon us."

This experience reminded me of one verse[2] from the book Gitanjali, written by the world-renowned author Sri Rabindranath Tagore, which I narrated to Susheela.

"A beggar was walking along begging, when he happened to see the king's chariot coming

---

[1] During the early years of the ashram, many ashramites often sent letters to Amma when she was away on foreign tours.
[2] The gist of verse 50, *Gitanjali*

towards him. He thought the king would remove his poverty and miseries instantly. But to the beggar's surprise, he saw the king holding out his right hand to him for alms. The beggar pondered for a moment; what a kingly jest it was. He stood confused and undecided, and then from his wallet he slowly took out the least little grain of corn and gave it to the king. At day's end he emptied his bag on the floor. To his great surprise, he found a least little grain of gold among the poor heap. He bitterly wept and wished that he had had the heart to give the king all."

Amma's divine way of healing the boil, and the mystic verse from Gitanjali in which the author has symbolically portrayed God as the king and the devotee as a beggar, filled Susheela's mind with a new awakening, and brought a visible transformation in her life. This unique experience also drew my mind nearer and nearer to Amma, helping me to surrender more and more to Her Divine Being.

Oṁ Namaḥ Śivāya

Oṁ Amṛteśwaryai Namaḥ

Chapter 8

Om Gāna-lolupāyai Namah[1]

Once, while Amma was giving darshan, a young man came and asked Her, "Isn't the bhajan singing on the stage a mere show?" Amma's quick answer was meant to be an eye opener for him. "Have you at any time been in love with someone? If so, you will understand the meaning of devotional singing. For a devotee, singing to God is like a heart-to-heart talk between the lover and the beloved."

---

[1] Salutations to the Divine Mother who delights in devotional music, Śrī Lalitā Sahasranāma Stotram, mantra 857

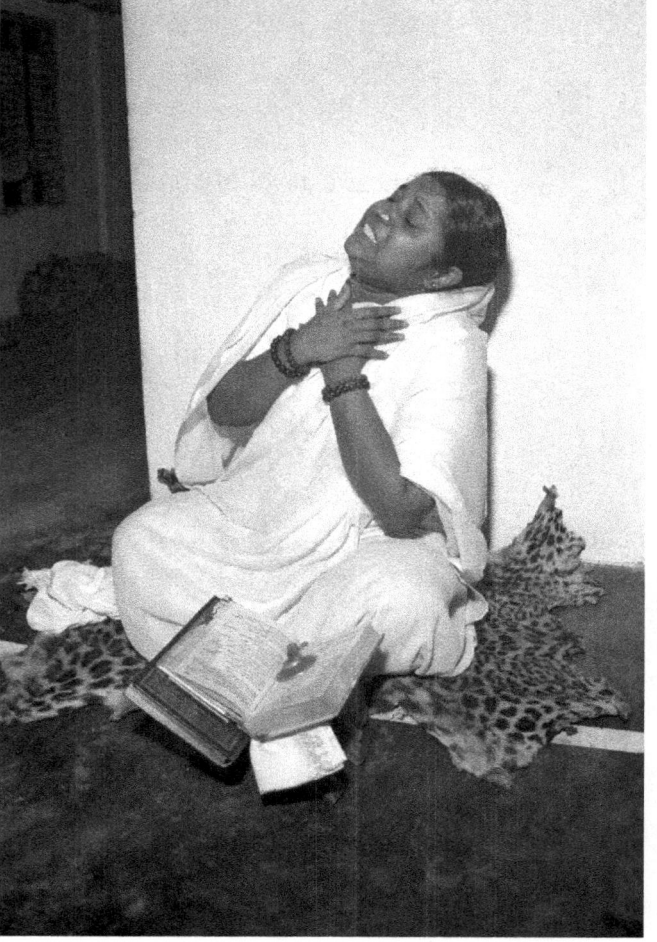

Millions of people who enjoy the Divine Mother's singing go beyond the bitter experiences of worldly life. To those who are exhausted by the scorching heat of day-to-day life in the world, these bhajans are like a life-giving shower of ambrosia. By Amma's grace, Dr. Rama, who was a devotee of Sri Krishna from childhood onwards, and later a close disciple of Amma, got an opportunity to experience the greatness of Amma's bhajans. One morning when Dr. Rama and I were engaged in conversation in my room, she asked me, *"Swaminiamma, if Amma is one with Sri Krishna, why does She sing bhajans to Him?"* Answering her question, I explained, "Like the sunlight which has many colours in it, Amma, the personification of Eternal Truth, has different divine forms in Her. Amma is praying to Bhagavan Sri Krishna for the sake of Her children, who, following Her example, can rid themselves of their worries and tensions from day-to-day life. For instance, occasionally Amma may tearfully sing, *Kanna niyenne marannuvoo* [Have you forgotten and forsaken me O, Kanna?], so that the devotees following Her example can enjoy divine bliss.

Following this conversation, Rama was blessed with a rare experience during the pre-bhava darshan bhajan at five o'clock in the evening, which revealed the true nature of Amma to her. As if Amma knew the whole of our conversation, She sang the very song, *Kanna niyenne marannuvoo?* Hearing the bhajan, Rama understood that Amma was revealing Her omniscience, true love and compassion to her. Afterwards, she spent the whole Bhava darshan night in Amma's holy presence with immense happiness. The next day Rama travelled to the hospital for her gallbladder surgery with unusual strength of mind. She was able to withstand the surgical procedure very well, though it happened to be a difficult one. Throughout the operation and postoperative period, Amma and the divine experience She gave were with Dr. Rama, facilitating her speedy recovery, and soon she could return to the ashram to continue her spiritual life with more vigour and energy. She became a good instrument in Amma's divine hands and often made donations to Amma for Her spiritual and humanitarian activities.

I was also inspired by the whole event which inspired me to write a song *Chitakasha seemayil annoru ghanashyama megham* [In the vast expanse of consciousness there appears the dense blue cloud, Sri Krishna] and offered the song at the sacred feet of Amma, who is *Sarva deva devi svarupini* [She Who has all the deities in Her].

The nectar of Amma's melodious singing flows to the devotees' hearts, enabling them to cross the barriers of narrow-mindedness. "Like the all-pervading space, Amma, who is inclusive of the whole world, is surely not affected by the walls raised between religious sects and ashrams," I thought to myself one evening while listening to Amma's bhajans in Amritapuri. As if agreeing with me completely, She immediately sang, *Martyare samsara varidhikkakkare, ettichitum Bhavatarini Ambike* [O, Ambika, who takes us across the ocean of worldly life]. When I heard the song, which was only occasionally sung by Amma and was originally from the *Gospel of Sri Ramakrishna*, once more I experienced Her omniscience and attitude of acceptance. I prayed wholeheartedly to Amma to enable me to take refuge in Her.

On a Bhava darshan day in Amritapuri I was talking to a few devotees. At that time, Gaurang, a high-school student, asked me, "My wish is to become the owner of a super-fast car; can I achieve it with Amma's help?" Since I had heard his parents often singing bhajans in Bengali, their mother tongue, I pointed out his mother to him and said, "If you sing bhajans like your parents, Amma will fulfil your wish. He replied, "Will Amma listen to my singing and give money for the car?" The anxiety and frailty of a teenager were in his question. I replied, "If you sing now, surely Amma will hear and even respond to it during the evening bhajans." Since he was still hesitating, I coaxed him, "My dear one, if you wish to have the car, sing the bhajans right now." Then he sang the Hindi song that begins,

Jago Ma Kali Jago,
Jago Ma Shyama Jago Jago

[Awake, Mother Kali, Awake, Mother Shyama!]

After a while they took leave of me. Soon after the evening bhajans started, I heard Amma singing *Jago Ma Kali*. I was delighted to think that by Amma's grace my words came true. The boy and his parents also cherished the memory of this rare experience. Later, Gaurang finished his higher education in Amma's institution and became the owner of not only a car, but also many material and spiritual achievements.

Oṁ Namaḥ Śivāya

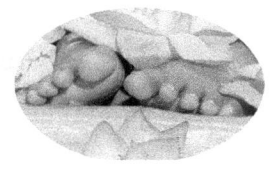

Oṁ Amṛteśwaryai Namaḥ

Chapter 9

Amma – Dhyāna-dhyātṛ-dhyeya-rūpā [1]

In the initial period, the ashramites stayed in thatched huts, constructed as per Amma's direction. Amma gave Bhava darshan in the small temple [kalari]. The usual daily darshan for devotees was given in a hut. After darshan was over, Amma permitted brahmacharini Lakshmi and me to stay in Her darshan hut. Since the hut had become old, it leaked here and there when it rained.

---

[1] The meditation, the meditator and the ideal of meditation, Śrī Lalitā Sahasranāma Stotram, mantra 254

One afternoon when I entered the hut I saw that the rainwater had collected on the floor near the door. Drops of water had fallen on one of the photographs of Amma. These drops shone like pearls on Her face. "Oh, my Mother is wet with rain water," I thought. Taking the photograph in my hand, I wiped off the drops of water from Amma's right cheek with my own cheek. After putting the picture lovingly back in its place, I wiped the floor with a mop and went for evening bhajans.

The next morning after meditation, I went to Amma's room to collect Her clothes for washing. When I climbed down the stairs with the bag of clothes, I saw Amma standing on the veranda of the meditation room on the ground floor. She graciously looked at me and made fun of me, calling, "dhobi, dhobi," (washerwoman). I was elated by the way Amma addressed me! When I reached near Her, Amma hugged me and closely kept her cheek on mine. For a moment I wondered what was the import of this unusual divine hug. But with Amma's blessings, soon I could connect it with what had happened the previous evening. I realized that Amma was responding to the service I had rendered to Her through the picture in Her own divine way, making me aware of Her holy presence in all Her pictures. I was overjoyed and prostrated at Amma's sacred feet, and took leave of Her.

Later in my ashram life I heard Amma cautioning the devotees, "It is not proper to burn Amma's photographs, since Amma's body will be affected by the heat. You can dispose of them by putting them in water."

Amma gave me another similar experience through one of Her photographs when I was walking through the courtyard of the ashram during the monsoon. At that time Amma was on a foreign tour. Unexpectedly, I saw a small photograph of Amma lying on the slushy ground. Immediately, I picked it up and looked at it. To my great surprise, I saw that the photograph was neither wet from the rain water, nor was it covered with mud. Soon, I recognised that it was one great lesson that Amma bestowed on me. A few minutes before I had seen the unusual photograph of Amma, I had sceptically thought of a divine experience Amma had had in her childhood. Amma had once told me that in Her childhood She had made a resolve to have a photograph of Sri Ramakrishna. Soon after, She saw one flowing towards Her through the backwater. Remembering this incident, which I had heard from Her directly, I had doubted for a moment, "How could a photograph come through the backwater unspoiled?" It was to make me free of this doubt that Amma had shown me that special photograph of Herself.

Amma the Creation, Creator and Power behind creation, gave me a similar experience on a later occasion. It was following the drastic tsunami on 26th of December 2004. The ashram yard and the ground floors of the ashram buildings were under the raging sea water for a while. I was in Haripad branch at that time and came to know of it through a phone call. Amma had given the rescue measures not only to the ashram, but also to all the affected areas. I prayed for those who suffered from the rage of Mother Ocean with the mantra, *"Lokah samastah sukhino bhavantu."* At that time a thought came to my mind about my personal belongings that were kept in my room at the Amritapuri ashram, and earnestly prayed, "Amma if they are all yours, kindly keep them safe." After a few days I understood that Amma had heard the prayer when I found my room and things, including books, were completely intact. This unique experience, which the Universal Mother imparted to me, was imprinted in my mind.

During my first year of ashram life, I experienced difficulty in choosing a form of meditation. Amma benevolently removed that difficulty through one of her photographs. In those days, the Divine Mother directly supervised our meditation, study of Vedanta, etc., and guided Her children according to their individual needs. Amma advised us to keep a picture of our beloved deity as an aid to our meditation, and not to switch from one to another. Though Amma had given me suggestions indirectly to cast away my slight confusion regarding the form of meditation, I was not able to put them into practice. After some days, I was going to my hut chanting the *Lalitā Sahasranāma* inwardly. When I reached my hut, the mantra, *dhyāna-dhyātṛ-dhyēya-rūpā* was in my mind. (I had reached that place in the Sahasranāma.) I simultaneously glanced at one of Amma's photographs hanging on the wall. Immediately I had an intuition that Amma was telling me, pointing to the picture, *"My dear child, this is your form of meditation; don't have any doubts hereafter."* It was a picture of Amma sitting in *ardha padmasana* (half-lotus posture) in *samadhi*[2]. Thereupon, I could fix my mind on Amma's divine words and the divine form that She revealed to me.

Amma is verily meditation, meditator and the meditated-upon (dhyāna-dhyātṛ-dhyēya-rūpā). "O, Amma, the indwelling Self, the embodiment of infinite bliss, kindly grant me incessant meditation on you," I prayed, and bowed down at Her lotus feet again and again!

Oṁ Namaḥ Śivāya

---

[2] The present altar picture in the meditation room where Amma was born.

www.ingramcontent.com/pod-product-compliance
Lightning Source LLC
Chambersburg PA
CBHW070633050426
42450CB00011B/3182

Breng spirituele waarden in de praktijk en red de wereld

Een toespraak van
Sri Mata Amritanandamayi
ter gelegenheid van de inauguratie
van de vieringen van de
150ste geboortedag van
Swami Vivekananda

Sirifort Auditorium, Nieuw Delhi
11 januari 2013

Mata Amritanandamayi Center, San Ramon
Californië, Verenigde Staten

Breng spirituele waarden in de praktijk en red de wereld

Een toespraak van Sri Mata Amritanandamayi
ter gelegenheid van de inauguratie van de vieringen
van de 150ste geboortedag van Swami Vivekananda
in het Sirifort Auditorium in Nieuw Delhi, India
op 11 januari 2013

Vertaald door Swami Amritaswarupananda

Uitgegeven door:
 Mata Amritanandamayi Center
 P.O. Box 613, San Ramon, CA 94583
 Verenigde Staten

––––––––– *Vivekananda Speech – Dutch* –––––––––

Copyright © 2013 door Mata Amritanandamayi Mission Trust, Amritapuri, Kerala 690546, India
Alle rechten voorbehouden. Niets uit deze uitgave mag worden opgeslagen in een geautomatiseerd gegevensbestand, verveelvoudigd, of openbaar gemaakt, in enige vorm of op enige wijze, hetzij elektronisch, mechanisch, door fotokopieën, opnamen, of op enige andere manier, zonder voorafgaande schriftelijke toestemming van de uitgever.

Eerste uitgave door het MA Center: mei 2016

In Nederland:
 www.amma.nl
 info@amma.nl

In België: www.vriendenvanamma.be

In India:
 www.amritapuri.org
 inform@amritapuri.org